CARRY ON

*An illustrated guide to what
you can and cannot take on your flight*

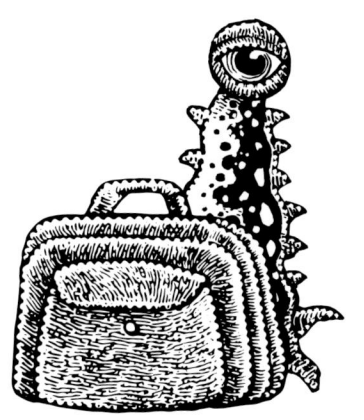

MORE THAN SEVENTY TIPS
ABOUT WHAT IS CONSIDERED SAFE
FOR CARRY-ON LUGGAGE.

Air travel consists largely of being extruded from one indignity and inconvenience to another. You may finally arrive somewhere—possibly your destination.

Written and illustrated by Don Moyer
so he'd have a excuse to draw ridiculous creatures doing absurd things.

Published by Calamity Worldwide LLC
612 Pennridge Road, Pittsburgh, PA 15211
www.calamityware.com

Copyright 2022 Don Moyer.
All rights reserved. No part of this publication may be reproduced or transmitted in any form or by any means, electronic or mechanical, without permission in writing from the copyright holder.
Exception: Reviewers are encouraged to reproduce portions of the book in conjunction with lavishly complimentary, positive reviews.
Email robot@calamityware.com.

Calamity number PT359
ISBN: 978-0-578-33332-8

First edition: February 2022
Printed and bound by inky wizards in China.

Special risks call for special care.

All travel is dangerous. But, because it attempts to defy gravity, air travel has special risks.

That's why experts have made lists of things that are safe and things that are too dangerous for you to take on your flight. This book is a visual summary of the highlights of that list.

For the latest rules and more detail, consult the website of the U.S. Transportation Security Administration.

Two warnings. First, checkpoint officers have the final say. If she wants to prohibit something you think is okay, you will lose that argument every time. Second, the airline's rules may be more restrictive. So, if you have concerns, check with them before you head for the airport with your chimpanzee, lasagna, or tuba.

DISCLAIMER

The advice in this book is intended
to help you pack wisely for your trip.
But, I may have made mistakes or
misunderstood the published guidelines.
The author bears no responsibility
whatsoever for errors in this book or
what happens when you travel
in the real world.
As always, you are on your own.
If your trip is inconvenient,
don't blame the advice in this book
and don't blame the author.
As always, I urge you to stay home.

Ready to go?

CARRY ON

Ammunition

No

CARRY ON

Antlers

Yes

CARRY ON

Axes and Hachets

No

CARRY ON

4

Baby Carriers

Yes

CARRY ON

5

Baby Food

Yes

CARRY ON

6
Balls

Yes
Soccer, basketball, baseball, football, tennis—all good.

CARRY ON

7

Baseball Bats

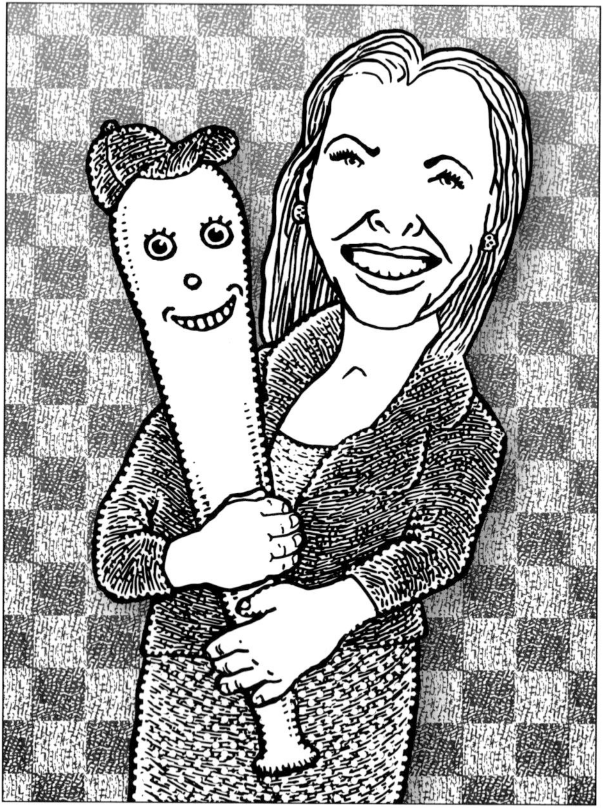

No

CARRY ON

Bear Spray

No

CARRY ON

Billy Clubs and Bludgeons

No

CARRY ON

Body Armor

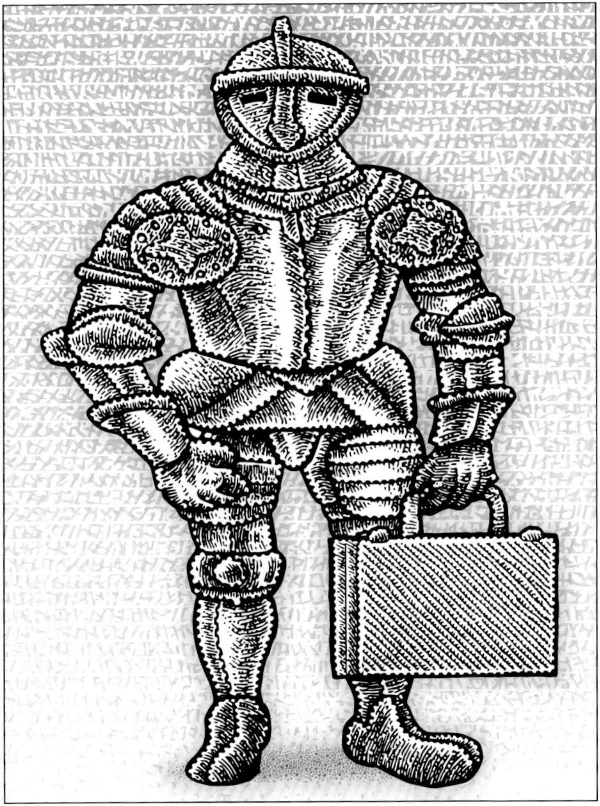

Yes

CARRY ON

11

Bowling Pins

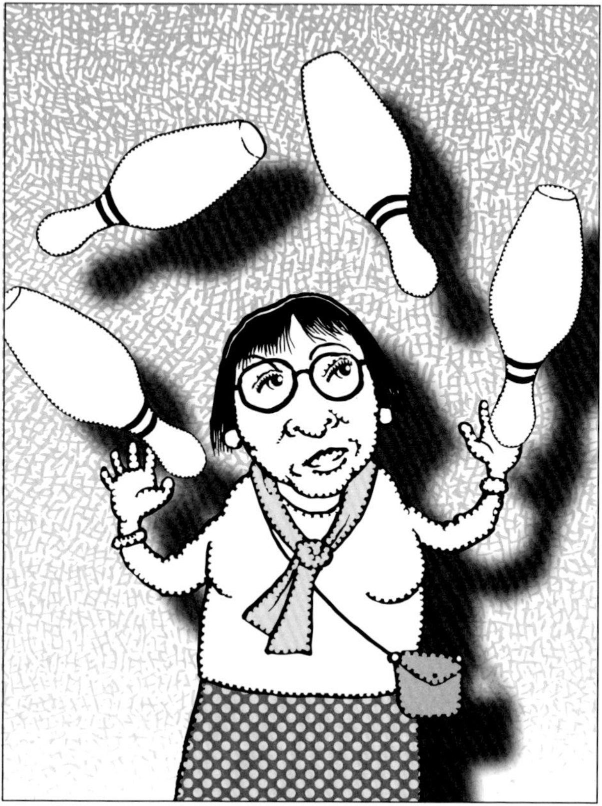

No

CARRY ON

12

Bows and Arrows

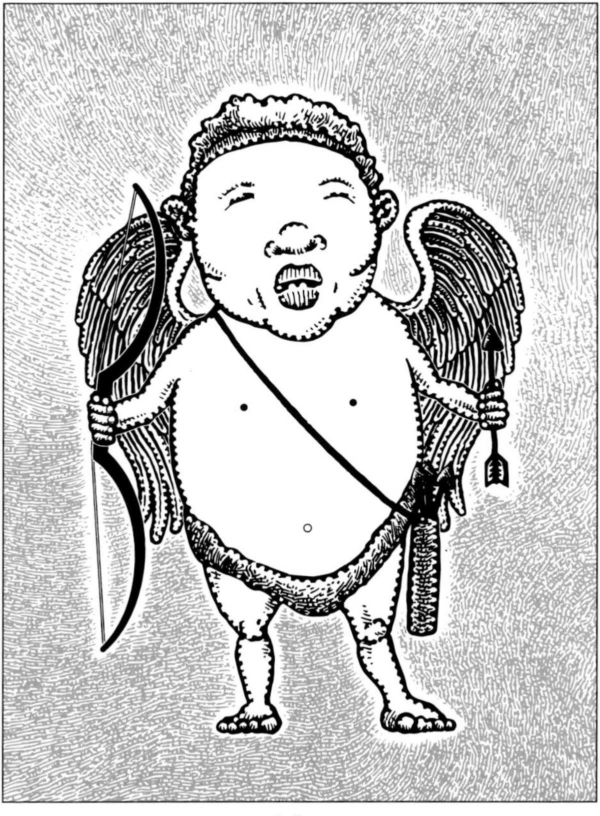

No

CARRY ON

⓭ Boxing Gloves

Yes

CARRY ON

Brass Musical Instruments

Yes
May need to fit under your seat. Check with the airline.

CARRY ON

Bug Repellent

No

CARRY ON

Candy

Yes

CARRY ON

Cattle Prods

No

CARRY ON

Cereal

Yes

CARRY ON

Cheese

Yes

CARRY ON

Christmas Lights

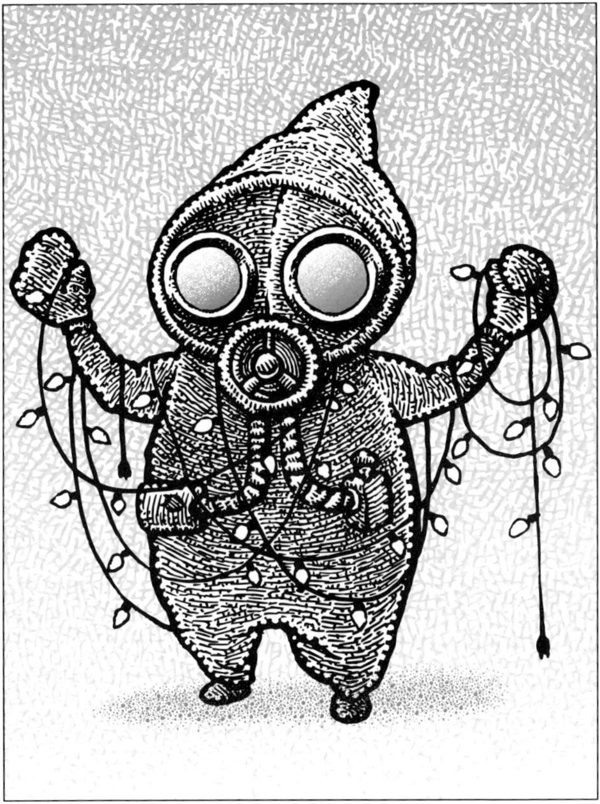

Yes

CARRY ON

Clocks

Yes

CARRY ON

Coat Hangers

Yes

CARRY ON

Coffee

Yes
Wait and buy a cup after you clear security.

CARRY ON

24

Crochet Hooks

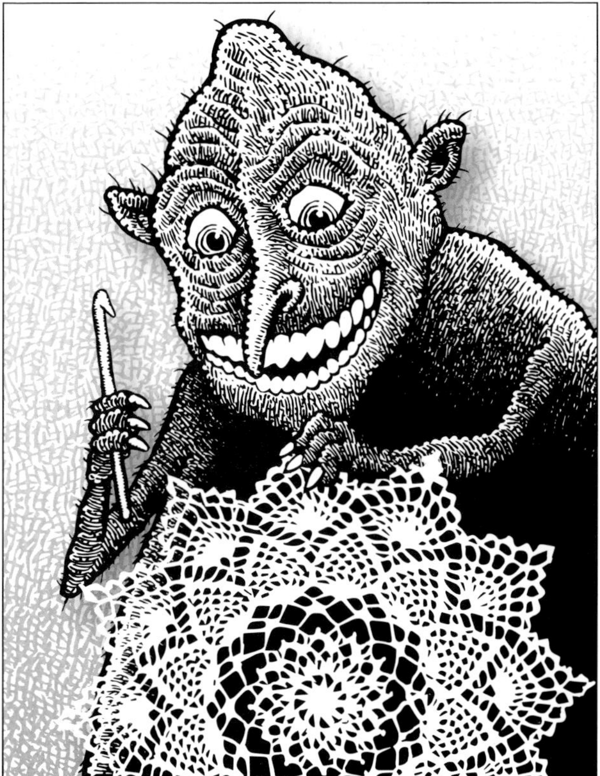

Yes

Knitting needles can come along too.

CARRY ON

Crowbars

No

CARRY ON

Crutches

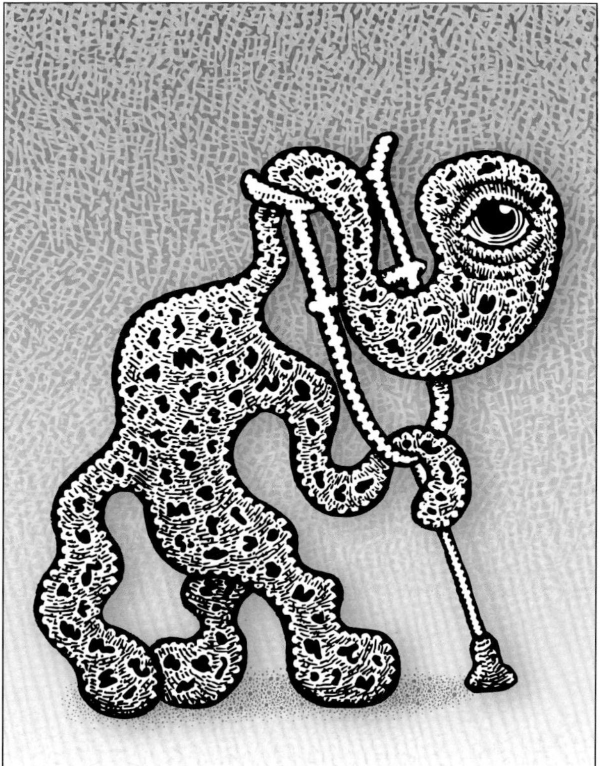

Yes

CARRY ON

Cymbals

Yes

CARRY ON

28

Dynamite

No

CARRY ON

Firearms

No

CARRY ON

Fireworks

No

CARRY ON

Forks

Yes

CARRY ON

Fresh Eggs

Yes

CARRY ON

33

Geiger Counter

Yes

CARRY ON

34

Hammers

Nope

CARRY ON

35

Handcuffs

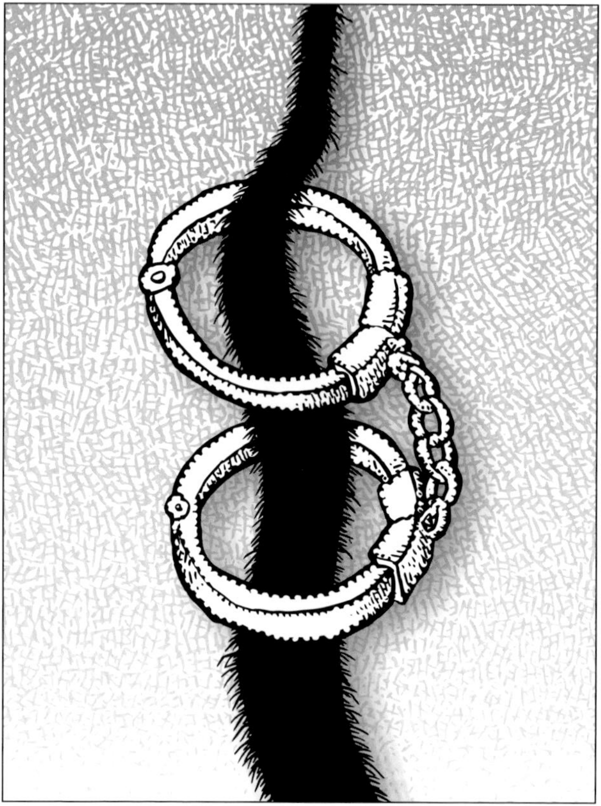

Yes

CARRY ON

36

Hand Grenades

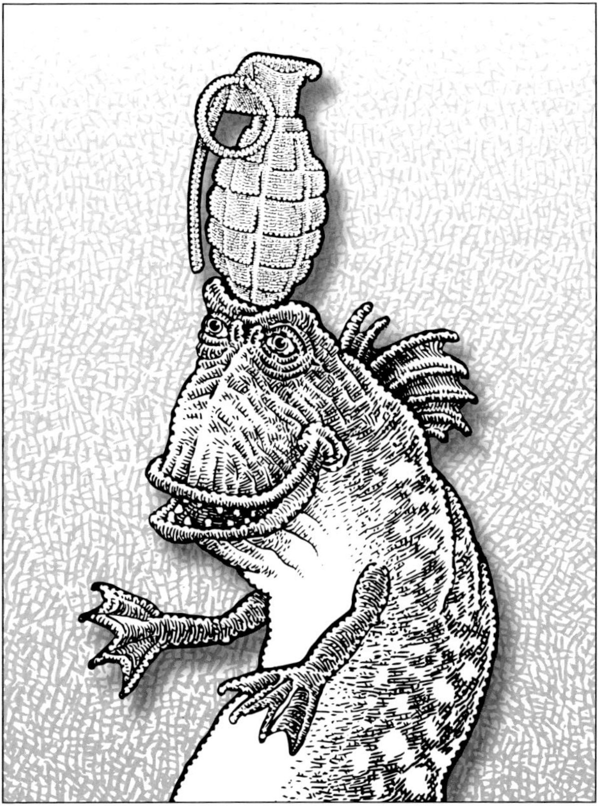

No

CARRY ON

37

Harry Potter Wands

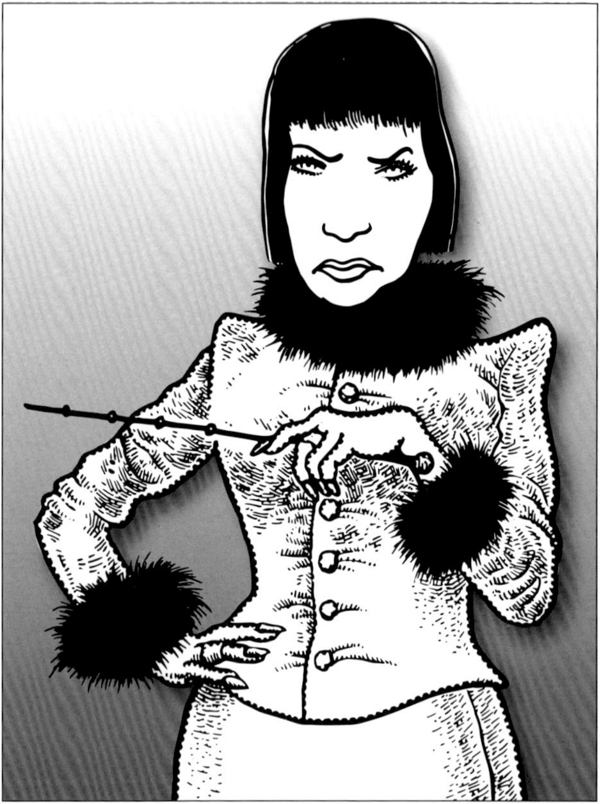

Yes

CARRY ON

Helmets

Yes

CARRY ON

Jewelry

Yes

CARRY ON

Knives

No

CARRY ON

41

Lasagna

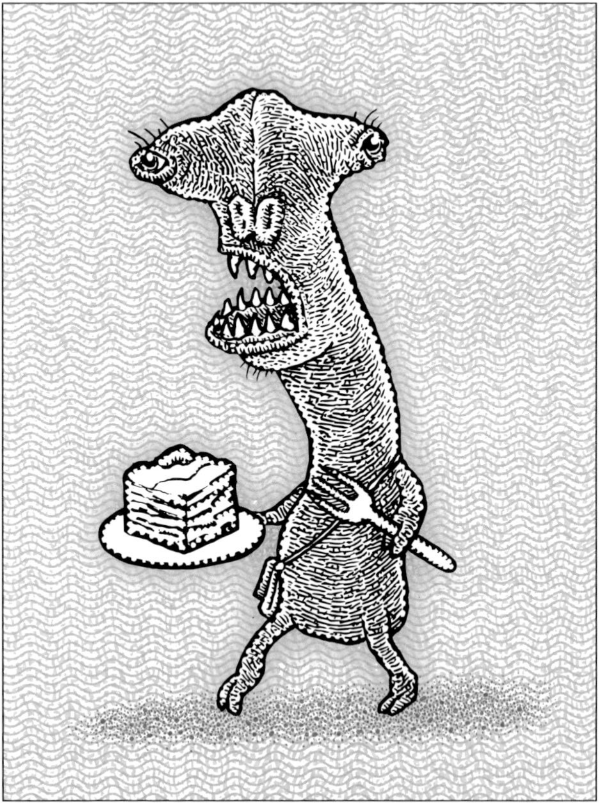

Yes, probably.

I must admit I'm guessing on this one.

CARRY ON

Lava Lamp

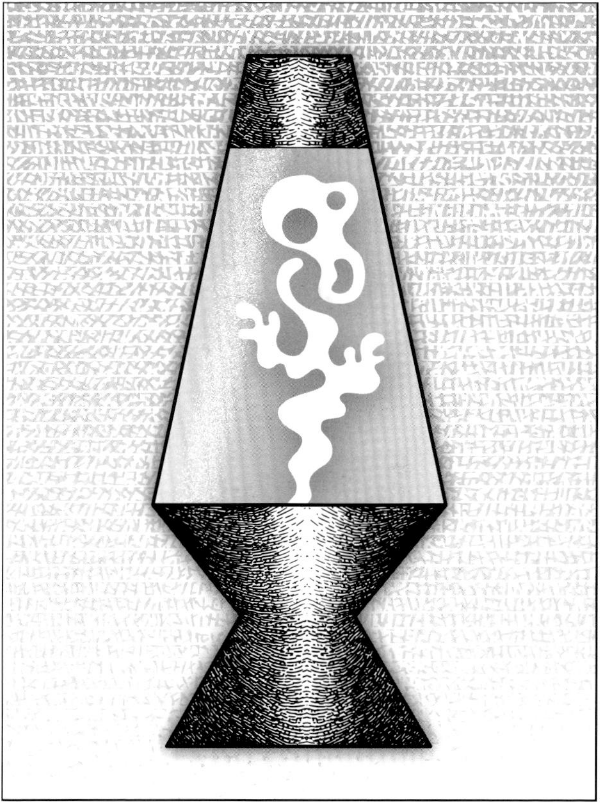

No

CARRY ON

43

Lightsaber

Yes

CARRY ON

Live Fish

Yes

CARRY ON

Lobster

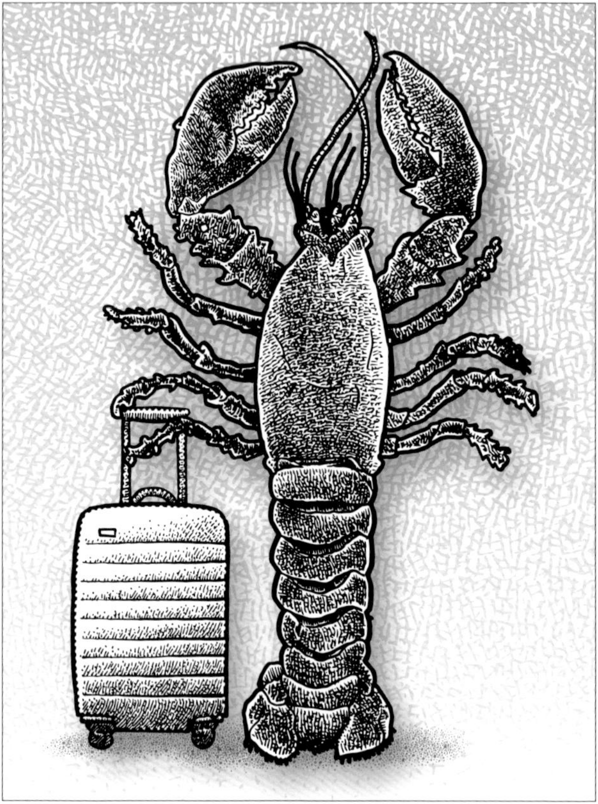

Yes

CARRY ON

Magic Eight Ball

No
But you probably already knew that.

CARRY ON

Mascara

Yes

You might as well look your best for the flight.

CARRY ON

48

Meat Cleavers

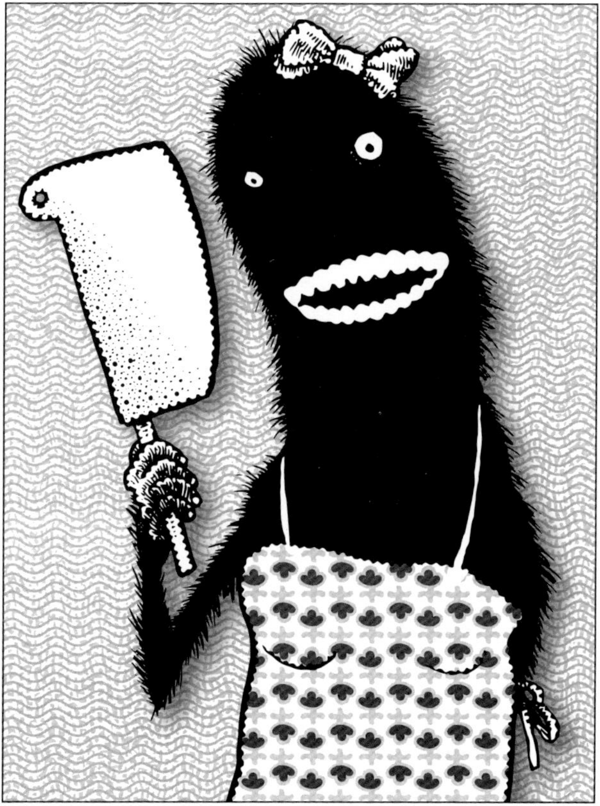

No

CARRY ON

Mirrors

Yes

CARRY ON

50

Nuts

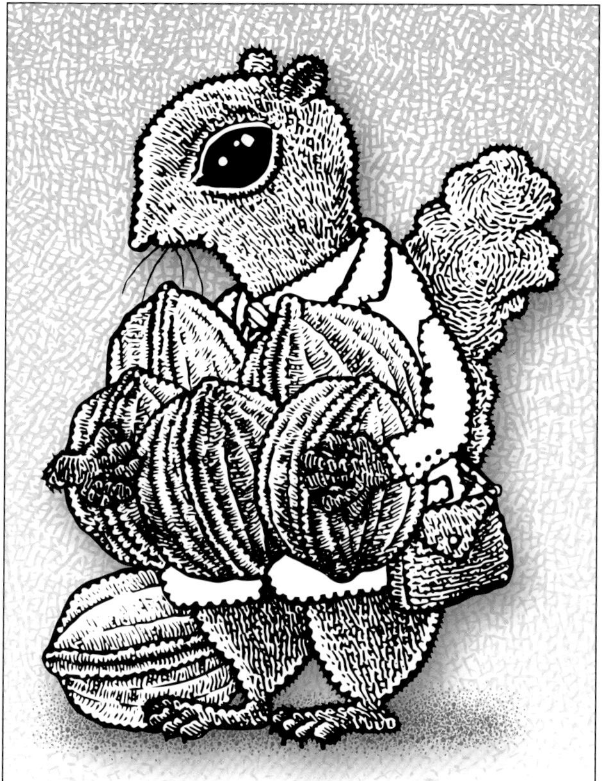

Yes

CARRY ON

Paintings

Yes

CARRY ON

52

Parachutes

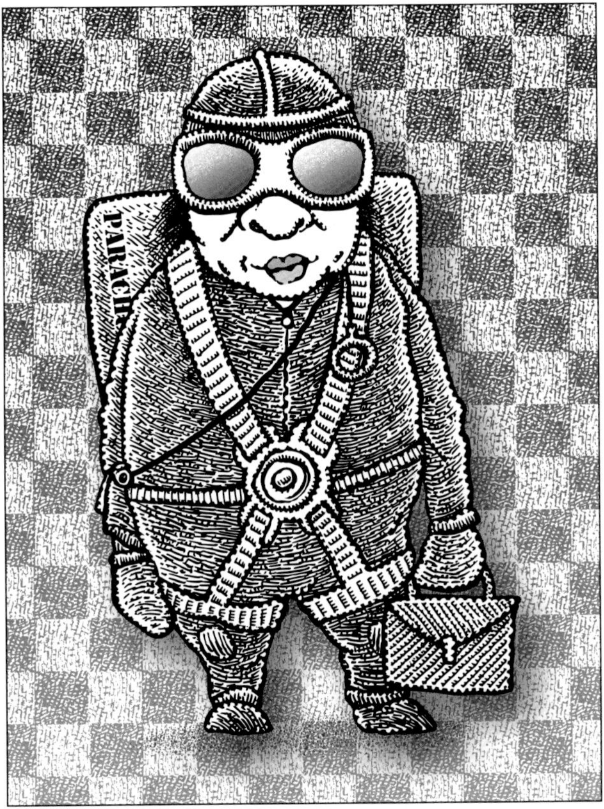

Yes, duh.

CARRY ON

Pizza

Yes

CARRY ON

Prosthetics

Yes

CARRY ON

Replicas of Firearms

Yes
Think obvious toys—squirt guns and the like.

CARRY ON

56

Rocket Launchers

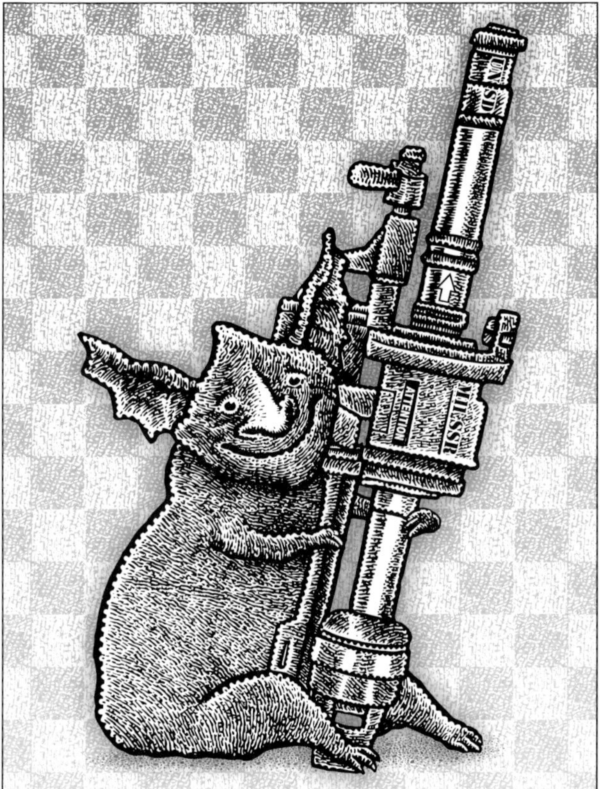

No

CARRY ON

Rocks

Yes

CARRY ON

Rope

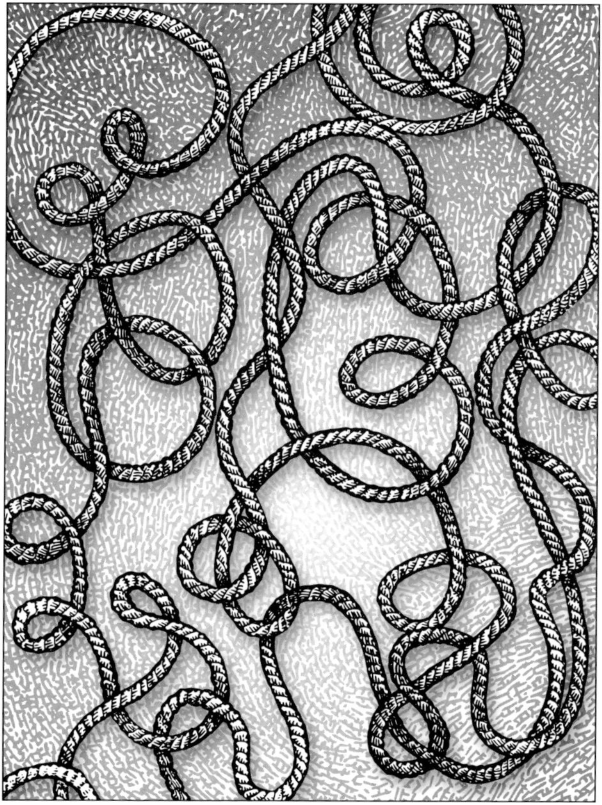

Yes

CARRY ON

59

Sandwiches

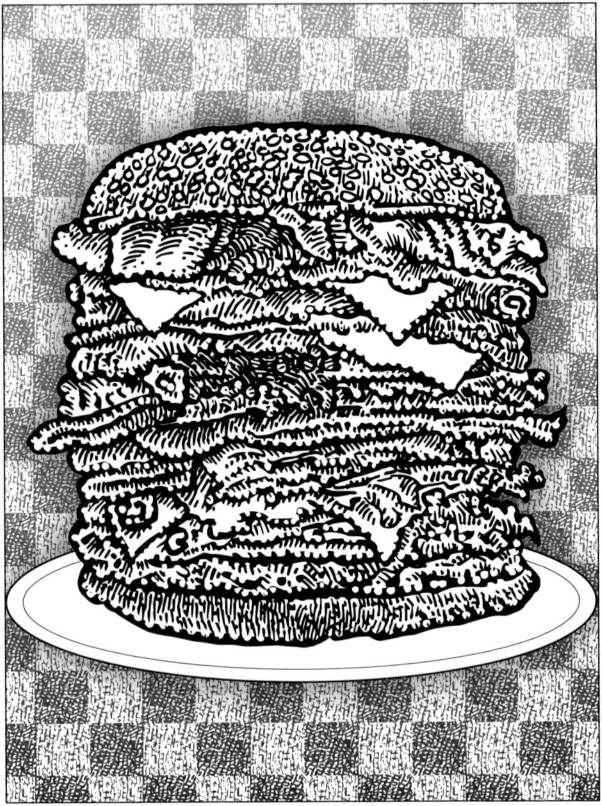

Yes

CARRY ON

Saws

No

CARRY ON

Scissors

Yes
Must measure less than 4 inches from pivot to tip.

CARRY ON

62

Shock Collars

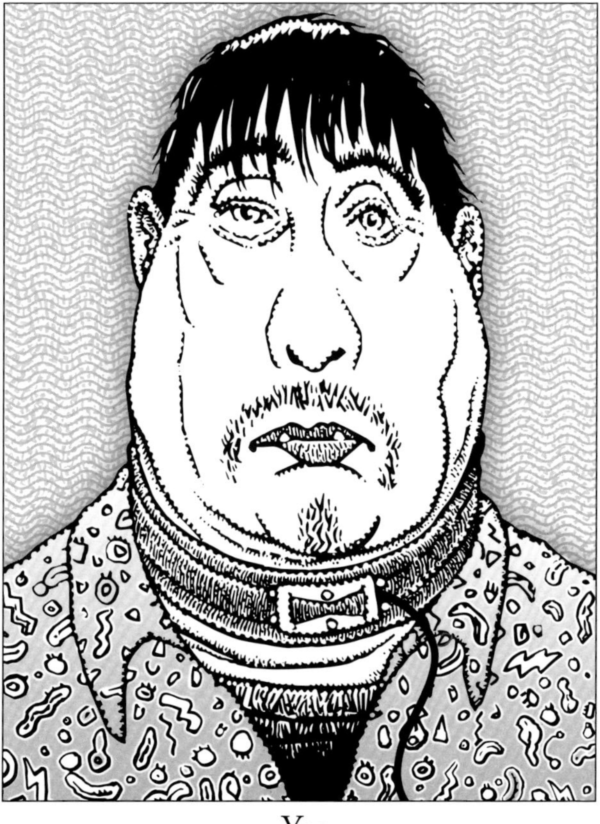

Yes

CARRY ON

Small Pets

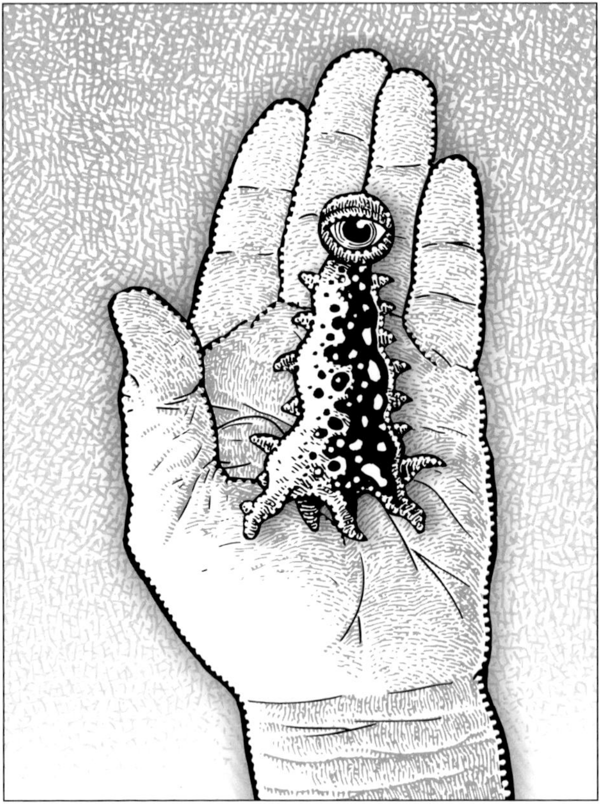

Yes
Check with airline for specific limitations.

CARRY ON

Snacks

Yes

CARRY ON

Snow Globes

Yes

Less than 3.4 ounces of liquid. Must fit inside quart-size bag.

CARRY ON

Snow Shoes

Yes

CARRY ON

Spear Guns

No

CARRY ON

68

Stuffed Animals

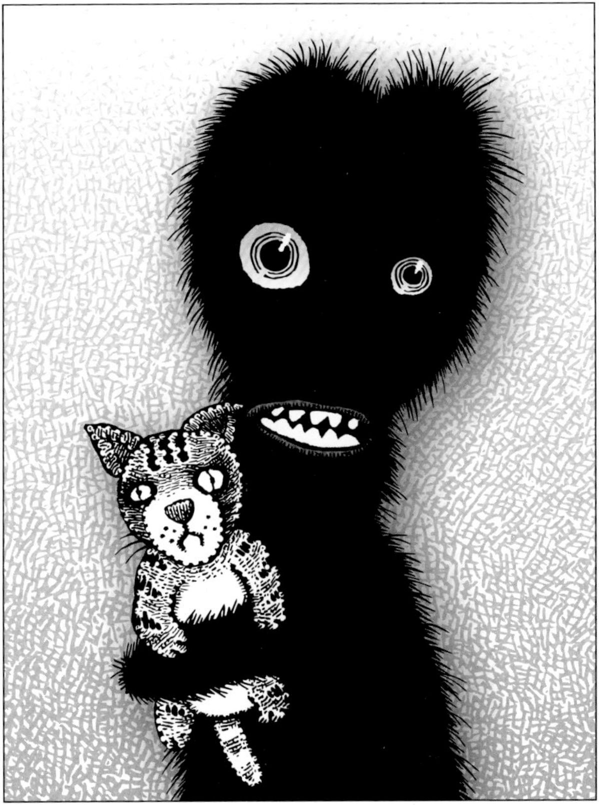

Yes

CARRY ON

Swords

No
No edged weapons—swords, sabers, daggers, rapiers, or knives

CARRY ON

70

Toy Robots

Yes

CARRY ON

71

Trophies

Yes

Congratulations on your win.

CARRY ON

Umbrellas

Yes

If you must go

There was a time when I flew for work almost every week. Now I don't. Staying home is far better. But if you can't avoid going to the airport, this book may help you cope with the anxiety of what to pack and what to leave behind. If I've done my job, you now know what to do with your axes, bludgeons, swords and hand grenades.

I hope your journey is worth the discomforts and inconveniences. Travel safely.

Don
Pittsburgh, February 2022

Acknowledgements

Special thanks for the brilliant help provided by Karen Moyer, Lynnette Kelley, Jack Kelley, Brandy Peightal, and Doris Zurawka.

Author

Don Moyer is a retired graphic designer with the freedom to indulge in self-inflicted projects, like this book. He draws a little every day. Don says, "I love to draw and the drawings I like best make me laugh." Don lives in Pittsburgh with The Amazing Karen.

Beautiful, useful, and funny

This book is one of the peculiar projects that emerged from the drawings in Don's sketchbooks. He's completed more than fifty of these efforts on Kickstarter and hopes to keep going. Discover more of these projects at www.calamityware.com, including Calamityware porcelain, textiles, books, letterpress prints, jigsaw puzzles, and the world's most charming shower curtain.